Original title:
Leafen Mires Within the Wizard Yolk

Author: Kene Elistrand
ISBN HARDBACK: 978-1-80563-436-2
ISBN PAPERBACK: 978-1-80564-957-1

The Twilight Symphony of Verdant Dreams

In twilight's glow, the shadows dance,
Beneath the leaves, where dreams entrance.
A whisper flows through emerald trees,
As night unfolds, a gentle breeze.

The stars ignite in silky skies,
While fireflies weave their soft replies.
Each note a secret, soft and clear,
In nature's choir, they draw us near.

A brook babbles in laughter's tune,
As silver night adorns the moon.
In every ripple, stories flow,
Of verdant paths where dreamers go.

With every sigh, the world awakes,
As twilight sings, the magic breaks.
A tapestry of green unfolds,
A symphony of dreams retold.

The night grows deep, yet still we stay,
To listen close to what they say.
For in this realm of softest night,
The verdant dreams take gentle flight.

Whispers of the Enchanted Glade

In twilight's hush, secrets weave,
A symphony that none perceive.
The fireflies flicker, tales untold,
Of magic born from leaves of gold.

Ancient trees stand tall and wise,
Guardians of dreams beneath the skies.
Their branches cradle whispers soft,
As shadows play in quiet loft.

A brook nearby sings ancient songs,
Where nature's heart forever longs.
With every ripple, memories dance,
In every glance, a secret chance.

The moonlight spills like liquid grace,
Illuminating every trace.
A gentle breeze stirs all around,
Where faded echoes can be found.

So linger here, in twilight lost,
For time stands still, and dreams accost.
In this glade, where spirits blend,
The whispers of magic never end.

Secrets of the Eldritch Grove

In shadows deep, where whispers hide,
Lies a grove where secrets bide.
The twisted roots, like fingers curled,\nEmbrace the
mysteries of the world.

Each leaf a tale, each wind a sigh,
In this realm where shadows lie.
The echoes murmur through the night,
Guarding tales of ancient light.

Flickering lights, like stars they dart,
Guiding the lost within the heart.
Where once the brave sought treasure's gleam,
Now lost within an endless dream.

The brook meanders, soft and low,
A source of wisdom, a thread to sew.
In every ripple, clarity flows,
As hidden knowledge gently grows.

So wander here, yet tread with care,
For magic lurks in stagnant air.
The secrets of the grove surround,
In eldritch whispers, truth is found.

Shadows Dance Among the Verdant Veils

In a realm where shadows twine,
Verdant veils dance, intertwine.
Mossy carpets, soft and lush,
Breathe life into the evening hush.

Amidst the ferns, the spirits fair,
Twist and turn in silver air.
From dappled light to twilight's haze,
The beauty holds in silent praise.

Moonbeams spill on emerald floor,
Tempting secrets to explore.
As laughter trails through leafy space,
A hint of magic leaves a trace.

But tread with care, for shadows play,
With whimsy bright and mischief gay.
In laughter's grasp, the night can twine,
A dance between the bold and fine.

So lose yourself in twilight's breath,
Feel the allure of shadowed depth.
Let whispers soft and moments rare,
Guide you through the magic there.

Beneath the Sparse Canopy

Beneath the sparse and flickering light,
Nature holds her secrets tight.
The branches sway, a soft embrace,
In hidden worlds, we find our place.

Gentle rustlings, whispers clear,
Voices lost but ever near.
In every pause, a heartbeat's sound,
A boundless magic dances round.

The forest speaks in colors bold,
Of memories that can't grow old.
Echoes of laughter, shadows cast,
In fleeting moments, futures past.

The clearing smiles with blooms that sway,
Each petal hints at a brighter day.
As sunlight filters, dreams take flight,
In scattered beams of magic light.

So, linger here where wonders bloom,
In sacred spaces, free of gloom.
Beneath the sparse and whispering trees,
Find solace in the gentle breeze.

Fantasies Shadowed by Verdancy

In a glade where whispers sigh,
And ferns like secrets creep,
The shadows dance on emerald leaves,
A realm where dreams still sleep.

Beneath the boughs, a tale unfolds,
Of creatures fair and bright,
Their laughter blending with the breeze,
In the soft and dappled light.

Yet doubt, like mist, can swirl the air,
Casting doubts on fledgling hopes,
A veil of shadows stirs the heart,
But still, the spirit copes.

Each petal holds a wish untold,
In colors bold and pure,
While nature's magic weaves the threads,
Of love, of joy, of cure.

So wander forth, where green confines,
And let your heart be free,
For in the woods, where shadows loom,
Lies the key to mystery.

The Alchemy of Roots and Branches

In tangled roots, the wisdom lies,
A network strong and wide,
With branches reaching for the skies,
In nature's arms, we bide.

The earth beneath, a sacred tome,
Of stories yet to tell,
Each leaf a page, each seed a home,
In this enchanted spell.

The sunbeams dance on dappled ground,
As whispers drift on air,
In every nook, a treasure found,
With secrets rich and rare.

A pot of gold at roots' embrace,
In shadows soft, we trust,
For magic thrives in hidden space,
Where hearts can dream and rust.

So gather close, in twilight's glow,
Let nature's charms unfold,
For in this alchemy we know,
The world is ours to hold.

Echoes of Whimsy in the Thicket

A laughter skips through twisted paths,
In thickets lush and sweet,
With every turn, a story weaves,
Where fantasy and nature meet.

Beneath the canopy's embrace,
The air is thick with mirth,
As sprites and fae in hidden place,
Reveal their joyful birth.

With gnarled branches pointing high,
To skies of azure hue,
Each echo sings a lullaby,
Of wonders fresh and new.

A world where whimsy knows no bounds,
Where imagination soars,
In every rustle, magic found,
And secret, whispered stores.

So step inside this thicket wild,
And let your spirit play,
For in this land, a merry child,
Shall chase the night away.

Illuminated Scrolls of the Green

In crumpled leaves, a treasure lies,
With secrets old and true,
Like scrolls of wisdom, penned by time,
In verdant shades of hue.

The light that filters through the trees,
A soft and glowing balm,
Illuminates the ancient script,
In nature's whispered calm.

Each rustle tells a tale of yore,
Of battles fought and won,
A journey through the forest's heart,
Where shadows blend with sun.

The emerald scrolls of green and gold,
Guide wanderers astray,
Through lands where dreams and truth unfold,
In wild, enchanting play.

So seek the magic in the glade,
Let stories rich ignite,
For in this realm where dreams are made,
The day surrenders night.

The Enigma of Gnarled Roots

In shadows deep, the secrets dwell,
Where ancient trees weave tales to tell.
Their roots like fingers, gripping tight,
Beneath the earth, away from light.

Whispers echo from the ground,
Of lost enchantments, softly found.
The gnarled limbs twist, bend, and sway,
In twilight's grasp, they softly play.

Creeping vines, a tapestry spun,
Guard treasures hid from the sun.
Each leaf a story, each branch a song,
In this enchanted realm, we belong.

The forest breathes, alive with lore,
Where shadows linger, mystery's door.
And those who seek with hearts sincere,
May find the truths that linger near.

So tread with care, and listen well,
For in these roots, the echoes dwell.
Gnarled and twisted, strong and wise,
The world of magic beneath the skies.

Sorcery and Silence at Dusk

As daylight fades, a hush descends,
The sun retreats, the night extends.
Moonlight spills on the whispering trees,
Awakens magic in the breeze.

Sorcery woven in twilight's grasp,
A gentle spell, a moonlit clasp.
With each soft shadow, secrets swirl,
In this serene and sacred world.

The owls hoot softly, a lullaby,
While stars sprinkle dreams across the sky.
A tranquil dance of night's embrace,
Where silence sings in a tranquil space.

Wands unfurl with a subtle glow,
Casting wonders, both high and low.
With every flick, the quiet sighs,
As magic stirs beneath the skies.

So take a breath, and close your eyes,
Feel the power, let thoughts arise.
In sorcery's heart, where silence reigns,
A world awaits, where all remains.

Underneath the Green Alchemy

Beneath the canopy, shadows bloom,
Where nature's whispers dispel all gloom.
Green alchemy swings on frail branches,
In the wild dance of leafy romances.

Ferns unfurl in an emerald haze,
Moss carpets ground in a soft embrace.
Life pulses gently, hidden and rare,
In this realm of wonder, dreams take air.

Potions brewed from the earth's sweet heart,
Nature's magic, a vital part.
With each small seed, a new tale breathes,
In the rustling leaves, the world believes.

Sunbeams pierce through the emerald sea,
Revealing wonders, wild and free.
Each creature shares the ancient lore,
Of life and love, forevermore.

So wander forth through the leafy maze,
Let the green marvels set you ablaze.
For underneath this alchemical dream,
Life flows in currents, a vibrant stream.

In the Realm of Emerald Whispers

In the heart of the wood, a secret sighs,
Emerald whispers beneath the skies.
Each leaf a promise, each branch a tale,
Where magic lingers, gentle and frail.

With every breeze, the stories flow,
Of ancient spirits, lost long ago.
In twilight's glow, old spells awake,
As shadows stretch, the silence breaks.

Dew-kissed petals, a fragrant spell,
Where the silence sings, all is well.
A dance of colors, vibrant and bright,
In the realm of whispers, day turns to night.

Sway with the trees, let go of doubt,
In emerald arms, let dreams sprout.
For in this place of quiet refrain,
The heart learns to dance, echoing plain.

So heed the call of the gentle trees,
Where emerald whispers drift on the breeze.
And with each step, feel the magic rise,
In this sacred realm, our spirits fly.

Echoing Spells of the Twilit Forest

Whispers weave through trees of gold,
Ancient tales in breezes told.
Moonlight shimmers on the glen,
Lurking spirits, hidden men.

Shadows dance in twilight's grace,
Mystic paths begin to trace.
Echoes of a world once bright,
Calling dreamers to the night.

Silvery fog, like velvet lace,
Wraps the forest in embrace.
Sparkling dew on emerald blades,
Where magic in the silence wades.

Through the bracken, softly tread,
Where ancient sorrows long have fled.
A symphony of sighs and charms,
Invites the heart to rest in arms.

Time stands still, in twilight's fold,
Every moment, a treasure to hold.
As echoing spells begin to rise,
The forest breathes under starlit skies.

The Green Embers of Forgotten Songs

In the heart of verdant glades,
Lies a rhythm that never fades.
Notes of laughter, soft and clear,
Dancing on the breeze we hear.

Whispers linger, tales untold,
Of haunted woods and heroes bold.
Each green ember, a spark divine,
Ignites the past, with roots entwined.

Lost in moments, time suspended,
Melodies that never ended.
Beneath the arching branches wide,
Where every song dares to abide.

Echoes of the softly strummed,
Fuse with twilight as they hum.
In every leaf, a story lies,
Beneath the vast, enchanted skies.

The green embers light our way,
Guiding us till break of day.
In the forest, we belong,
As we sing the forgotten song.

In the Heart of Verdant Enchantment

Where the wildflowers softly bloom,
In the air, a sweet perfume.
Colors dance in gentle sway,
Whispering secrets of the day.

Winds of fortune sweep the vale,
Carrying tales on a delicate trail.
The heart beats in whispered cheer,
Echoing dreams that linger near.

In the deep of twilight's hue,
Magic stirs and finds its due.
Every shadow, every glint,
Holds a spell, a soft imprint.

Cascading light through branches high,
Calls to spirits passing by.
In this realm of lush delight,
Everything feels just right.

In the heart of green enchantment,
Lies the essence of our contentment.
Where nature's grace and dreams align,
We find a world, forever divine.

The Witches' Retreat in the Underbrush

Hidden deep within the pine,
Where shadows dance and moonlight shines.
The witches gather for their rites,
Whispered spells beneath the nights.

In the underbrush, secrets lay,
Brewing potions in the play.
Herbs and whispers twine and weave,
Crafting wonders to believe.

Cauldrons bubble, embers glow,
As the ancient magic flows.
Nature's chorus hums along,
In this sheltered, sacred throng.

Leaves remember every laugh,
A tapestry on nature's path.
Through the thicket, echoes ring,
Of a truth the wild can bring.

In the heart of the creeping vine,
Witches brew their fateful line.
A retreat hidden from the light,
In the underbrush, all feels right.

Secrets of the Elven Grotto

Deep in the woods where shadows play,
Whispers of magic drift and sway.
Elven songs in twilight hum,
Guarding secrets for those who come.

Crystals gleam in the soft moonlight,
Fires flicker, casting dreams so bright.
Hidden paths of endless lore,
Await the brave who seek once more.

Ancient trees with wisdom old,
Guard their tales, both fierce and bold.
In this realm where dreams are spun,
Each moment holds a fateful run.

Glittering waters, clear as glass,
Reflecting tales of those who pass.
Time stands still in this sacred place,
Bound by enchantment's sweet embrace.

Yet beware the twilight's tease,
For not all spirits find their ease.
In the Grotto where shadows are cast,
Some secrets are meant to remain fast.

Timeless Adrift in Leaf Light

Under the boughs where the sunlight plays,
Dancing on leaves in whimsical ways.
Time drifts softly, a feathered sigh,
Held in the hush of an azure sky.

Golden rays through the branches peek,
Whispering wonders, delicate and weak.
Moss-clad stones in the gentle air,
Harbor stories, both rich and rare.

Glimmers of laughter entwined with breeze,
Carried away through the towering trees.
Each leaf a memory, fragile and bright,
Held in the warmth of the fading light.

Moments eternal in the grove's embrace,
Time unravels, a slow-motion race.
In this sanctuary where soft winds sigh,
Life blooms forever; it knows not to die.

Adrift in wonder, the heart takes flight,
Beneath the canopy, the world feels right.
Wrapped in the glow of the leaf's delight,
Timeless we wander, in pure moonlight.

Wandering Spirits of the Grove

In shadows deep where the wild things roam,
Spirits whisper, far from home.
Fleeting forms in the quiet mist,
Guarding dreams that none can list.

Echoes of laughter, forgotten song,
In the grove where the lost belong.
With each rustle of the ferns so green,
Wandering spirits weave unseen.

Soft golden glows through the branches fall,
Illuminating secrets, embracing all.
With each gentle breeze, old tales revive,
As night draws close, the dreams arrive.

Magic lingers, breathes in the night,
Twinkling softly, a siren's light.
In this woodland where shadows blend,
Time is a thread that knows no end.

So listen closely, let your heart feel,
For wandering spirits are ever real.
Among the trees, where shadows weave,
You'll find the magic that you believed.

Enchanted Paths in Sylvan Realms

Through emerald halls where the sunlight bends,
Lie enchanted paths that never end.
Whispers of hope on the winding trail,
Promising magic where dreams prevail.

Each footstep taken in twilight's glow,
Treads on the mysteries, few truly know.
The air alive with spells that twine,
In sylvan realms where fates align.

Misty morning, a soft embrace,
Brushing through time and infinite space.
Ancient echoes in each gentle breeze,
Calling forth truths beneath the trees.

With every shadow that dances near,
Legends of old awaken our fear.
Yet in the glimmers of soft moonlight,
Lie paths to take, paths of delight.

Come wander the woods, where magic flows,
In enchanted realms where the heart knows.
For every step you bravely take,
Leads you to wonders that dreams can make.

The Confluence of Magic in Moss

In a glen where shadows weave,
Moss blankets earth with ancient tales.
Flickers of light begin to leave,
As whispers dance on soft green veils.

Beneath the oak, where secrets hum,
A tapestry of life unfolds.
With every step, a gentle thrum,
The heart of magic, pure and bold.

Crystals form in morning's dew,
Nature's gems upon the ground.
In silence born, the world renews,
In mossy beds, the lost are found.

With tendrils soft and colors bright,
The forest breathes a song so sweet.
Embrace the dawn, embrace the night,
In every step, magic's heartbeat.

As leaves above begin to sway,
The symphony of life ignites.
In this enchanted, mossy play,
Old stories weave through golden lights.

Reverberations of the Wild Unknown

In echoes wild, the forest sings,
A song that stirs the shadows deep.
Each footfall wakes forgotten things,
In whispers dark, the night won't sleep.

The branches twist like ancient lore,
With secrets wrapped in twilight's breath.
In every rustle lies the core,
Of life and death, of love and death.

Beneath the stars, the spirits roam,
In dancing flames, in whispers low.
Each heartache finds a hidden home,
Where silence speaks, where wild winds blow.

Through tangled roots and crystal streams,
The pulse of nature draws us near.
In every breeze, the wild seems,
To beckon forth without a fear.

Yet tread with care, for unseen eyes,
Observe the wanderer's delight.
In beauty, danger often lies,
In moonlit realms where dreams take flight.

The Enchanted Tangle of Nature's Fingers

In lush embrace, the branches twist,
Nature's hands create a maze.
Each foliage touch, a gentle kiss,
As sunlight weaves through leafy haze.

The vines entwine like lovers' dreams,
With whispers soft as evening's sighs.
In every curl, a magic beams,
That captivates the wandering eyes.

A dappled path, a winding fate,
Where each step leads to worlds anew.
In tangled realms, we hesitate,
For beauty blooms in shades of blue.

From petals bright to roots so old,
The earth reveals its sacred truth.
In every groove, a tale retold,
Of wisdom wrapped in nature's youth.

So lose yourself in wild embrace,
In every turn, a life to chase.
For in this tangle, hearts will race,
With nature's fingers, find your place.

A Canvas of Whispers and Leaves

A canvas spread of green and gold,
Where art is born in nature's hand.
Each leaf a story yet untold,
In every breath, the world can stand.

With every rustle in the breeze,
A paean sung through time and space.
In shadows' dance, the mind finds ease,
As whispers swirl in nature's grace.

The colors shift with sun and shade,
A masterpiece that shifts and flows.
In every inch, a craft is laid,
Where beauty's pulse forever grows.

The canvas breathes; it lives, it sighs,
In hues of emerald, clay, and sky.
Each stroke of wind, a sweet surprise,
A tender heart that longs to fly.

So wander through this vivid realm,
Where leaves become the brush of dreams.
In every glance, take up the helm,
And paint your song with whispered themes.

Threads of Fate in Foliar Fibers

In the whispering woods where secrets hide,
Threads of fate in fibers glide.
Leaves entwined with mysteries old,
Stories whispered, waiting to unfold.

Nature weaves a tapestry rare,
With each thread spun in gentle air.
A tapestry rich, yet finely spun,
Binding the earth to the crimson sun.

Beneath the boughs where shadows play,
Paths entwine in a vibrant display.
Nature's loom in a vibrant dance,
Invites the heart to take a chance.

In twilight's glow, the colors bloom,
Filling the woods with sweet perfume.
Each strand a tale of heart's desire,
Stitched in the night by fate's own fire.

So wander here, and lose your fears,
In the forest's embrace, dry your tears.
For the threads of fate are spun with care,
In the leaves above, you're bound to share.

Spells Cast on Sylvan Breezes

From the depths of woods where shadows loom,
Spells are cast on the sylvan gloom.
Whispers rise on the gentle breeze,
Waking the magic in the trees.

With a flick of leaves and a rustling sigh,
The spirits of old begin to fly.
Chords of enchantment fill the air,
A melody sweeter than anything rare.

Moss carpets the ground, lush and green,
It holds the secrets that remain unseen.
In the twilight hour, the spells are spun,
Dancing with fireflies, one by one.

Branches stretch high, embracing the night,
While moonbeams twinkle with silver light.
Each gust of wind reveals a thought,
In the embrace of the dark, we are caught.

So listen closely to the sighs of trees,
For they speak in the rustle of leaves.
Spells cast forth on the sylvan breeze,
Will weave you into the forest's tease.

The Oracle's Shade Beneath the Trees

In the glade where secrets dwell,
Lies the oracle with tales to tell.
Beneath the trees, where shadows blend,
Life's needful truths and time suspend.

Gnarled roots twist with wisdom's grace,
In this enchanted, sacred space.
Gaze into the pools of her knowing eyes,
Where the past and future quietly lie.

Leaves whisper softly, secrets held dear,
As she calls forth what you might fear.
Each prophecy cloaked in gentle shade,
Gives strength to journeys that fate has made.

Branches encircle, a fortress unseen,
Keeps the weight of the world serene.
So heed her words, and take your time,
For in her shade, all is sublime.

With each soft echo, hearts may sway,
In the shade of truth, find your way.
The oracle waits with arms open wide,
Beneath the trees where dreams abide.

When Moonlight Kisses Moss

When moonlight kisses the velvet moss,
Glittering softly, causing no loss.
A world wrapped in silvery dreams,
As nature glimmers and subtly gleams.

Each droplet glistens like a jewel fair,
Night's quiet moments hang in the air.
Underneath the stars, shadows dance,
In the moon's embrace, find your chance.

Whispers travel on the evening's breath,
Echoes of life, a celestial wreath.
The night unfolds like a magic scroll,
Revealing wishes deep in the soul.

Through the tranquil leaves, the stars will weave,
A spell of peace that one can believe.
In every shimmer, a secret glows,
As time stands still where moonlight flows.

So linger here, let the heart align,
With the soft caress of the night's design.
For in this moment, lost and found,
The whispers of the night will abound.

Dance of the Fae in Woodland Glimmers

In twilight's glow, the fae appear,
They twirl and sway with joy sincere.
Beneath the leaves, their laughter sings,
As moonlight whispers, gentle wings.

With every step, the shadows play,
The forest hums a soft ballet.
In silvered pools, the starlight gleams,
Where dreams and nature weave their seams.

Around the trees, their magic flows,
In secret paths, a world that knows.
A flicker here, a shimmer there,
The fae rejoice—no heart can scare.

As dawn draws near, they take their flight,
To hidden realms, beyond our sight.
But in our dreams, they still remain,
In woodland glimmers, soft as rain.

So if you listen, soft and clear,
You'll sense their dance, you'll feel them near.
In every rustle, in every sigh,
The fae are near; they never die.

The Hidden Map of Nature's Graces

Beneath the rustling leaves of green,
A map of wonders waits unseen.
Each brook and stone has tales to weave,
A gift for those who dare believe.

The whispers of the ancient trees,
Are guiding lights upon the breeze.
With every step, a secret shared,
A bond with nature, gently dared.

The petals bloom with colors bright,
In morning's dew, they catch the light.
Each path we walk, a timeless song,
Where roots of earth and dreams belong.

So heed the signs, the patterns clear,
Nature's grace draws ever near.
With every leaf, there lies a clue,
A hidden world for me and you.

In silent groves, let wonders spark,
As echoes linger in the dark.
A treasure map, both old and new,
In nature's arms, we find what's true.

Unveiling the Secrets of Silent Canopies

In secret woods, the canopies sway,
Where mysteries dance in the softest play.
Hidden voices in shadows call,
To share their stories, one and all.

With every rustle, a tale divine,
Of magic spun from the ancient vine.
In twilight's glow, the truth unfolds,
In whispered dreams, the forest holds.

Through tangled boughs, the sunlight streams,
Awakening hushed and tender dreams.
Each leaf a page, each breeze a sigh,
In silent canopies, time flits by.

The creatures tread on paths unseen,
Guardians of the woods and green.
With patient hearts, the secrets share,
Of lives entwined, beyond compare.

So wander deep, where magic waits,
In the heart of forest's gates.
As twilight dims and stars ignite,
The secrets weave in the cloak of night.

Woven Threads of Nature's Magic

In nature's loom, the colors blend,
A tapestry where worlds descend.
With each soft thread, a story found,
In whispers woven into the ground.

The rivers stitch the hillsides tight,
Binding the earth in soft twilight.
A dance of roots, a song of skies,
Where dreams are born, and magic lies.

From blossoms rare, to shadows deep,
The threads of life in silence creep.
With every breeze, the weavings sway,
Crafting the night from edge of day.

In this grand fabric, hearts entwine,
Each heartbeat echoes, pure, divine.
The dreams of ancients, hopes and fears,
Unravel softly through the years.

So take a moment, breathe it in,
The magic crafted, none can win.
In nature's threads, behold the art,
A woven wonder, a beating heart.

Flickers in the Twilight Canopy

Beneath the stars, the shadows play,
Whispers of magic drift away.
Owls call softly, the night is young,
In twilight's embrace, old tales are sung.

Breezes weave through the ancient trees,
Carrying secrets on the gentle breeze.
Moonbeams dance on the forest floor,
A tapestry of dreams, forever more.

Mossy stones with stories to tell,
Each one holds a spell, all cast so well.
Flickers of light in the growing dark,
Igniting the woods with a spark.

Creatures stir in the cozy night,
Chasing shadows in playful fright.
Leaves will whisper, rustle and sigh,
In the canopy where the dreams fly high.

As dawn approaches, shadows retreat,
With the sun's kiss, the magic's sweet.
Yet in the heart of the sleeping wood,
Flickers of twilight, forever stood.

The Sorceress's Grotto of Green

In a hidden nook, where the wildflowers grow,
A sorceress wanders, with secrets to show.
Her laughter is wrapped in the emerald leaves,
Guarding the magic that nature conceives.

Crystals shimmer in the cool, damp air,
Casting rainbows that glisten with flair.
With a flick of her wrist, the vines intertwine,
Creating a haven, both tranquil and divine.

Echoes of spells weave through the trees,
As creatures gather, enchanted with ease.
Her potion brews in a cauldron of clay,
Infusing the grotto with golden rays.

Moonlight drapes over the sylvan scene,
Painting the night with a silvery sheen.
In shadows, a dance of fae begins,
A celebration where magic spins.

When twilight wanes and the stars ignite,
The sorceress whispers, bidding goodnight.
Yet in her grotto, forever shall be,
An echo of wonder, wild and free.

A Symphony of Leaves and Lore

In the golden light of an autumn day,
Leaves flutter down in a graceful sway.
Whispers of tales from long ago,
Rustle among them, in the wind they flow.

Each leaf a story, a memory spun,
Of heroes and dreams, and battles won.
The trees stand tall, guardians of time,
Their roots entwined in an ancient rhyme.

Beneath the boughs, the world feels anew,
As sunlight filters and rainbows break through.
A symphony plays, sweet and sublime,
Nature's own music in rhythm and rhyme.

As twilight descends, the shadows grow deep,
Stars peek through branches, their watch they keep.
The symphony lingers, so soft and pure,
A promise of magic that will endure.

In every rustle, in every sigh,
The leaves tell stories, as time passes by.
A tapestry woven with whispers and lore,
In the heart of the forest, forevermore.

Everlasting Whispers of the Glade

In the heart of the glade where the wildflowers bloom,
Soft whispers echo, dispelling all gloom.
The flutter of wings and the rustle of grass,
Hold secrets of ages that none can surpass.

Here time stands still, in a dance so divine,
With each gentle breeze, a magical sign.
The echoes of laughter, of joy and of pain,
Are held in the glade where memories reign.

Sunlight streams through the canopy bright,
Embracing the shadows, chasing the night.
Leaves sway in rhythm, a soft lullaby,
In the whispers of nature, where dreams learn to fly.

As dusk gently falls, the fireflies gleam,
Igniting the glade with a shimmering dream.
Everlasting whispers paint stories so bold,
In the heart of the forest, where magic unfolds.

Each breath of the wind carries time's gentle kiss,
A promise of peace, a moment of bliss.
In the glade, softly woven, forever it stays,
A sanctuary of magic, where nature's heart plays.

Whims of the Wind in Ancient Boughs

In whispering winds, the secrets lie,
Beneath the leaves, where shadows sigh.
The ancient boughs, they twist and turn,
With tales of magic, both bright and stern.

A dance of whispers, the trees conspire,
As dreams take flight, like sparks of fire.
They beckon softly, to those who dare,
To seek the wonder lurking there.

Beneath the moon, their voices swell,
Entwined in stories no tongue can tell.
Each sigh, each creak, a timeworn song,
A melody where we all belong.

In twilight's grasp, the magic hums,
With every heartbeat, the mystery drums.
A world of wonders, both lost and found,
In ancient boughs, where dreams abound.

So step within this verdant dome,
Where every path may lead you home.
Embrace the whims of the wind, so free,
In ancient boughs, just you and me.

Oaths Cast in Bark and Berry

In glades where sunlight dapples gold,
Oaths are whispered, brave and bold.
Bark and berry hold the tales,
Of promises made, and love that prevails.

The roots entwined, a sacred bond,
In nature's arms, our spirits respond.
With every bloom, our vows take flight,
In fragrant whispers of day and night.

The wildflower's grace, a hand in hand,
Two hearts united, strong as the land.
With every season, our pledge renews,
In quiet moments, love's truth we choose.

So gather round, let the stories pour,
Of oaths cast deep, forever more.
In the rustling leaves, a promise rings,
In bark and berry, our spirit sings.

Through rain and storm, our roots remain,
Beneath the sky, we share the pain.
Yet through the dark, the light will shine,
In sacred oaths, your heart is mine.

Tides of Magic in the Foliage

In leafy realms, where secrets churn,
The tides of magic rise and burn.
Hidden glimmers, in shadows cast,
Whispers of wonders, from ages past.

Beneath the ferns, the stories flow,
Of ancient spirits, row by row.
The roots entwined in mystic dance,
In every rustle, a timeless chance.

A flicker of light, a shadow's grace,
In nature's heart, find your place.
The magic weaves through arching vine,
Connecting souls, both yours and mine.

In twilight's glow, the shadows sing,
Of all the joy and love they bring.
So walk with me in this leafy sea,
Where tides of magic set us free.

The world is vast, yet small it feels,
As every heartbeat, the wonder reveals.
In every leaf, a spark ignites,
In tides of magic, our dreams take flight.

The Realm Where Shadows Blossom

In the quiet corners of the night,
Where shadows stir, and dreams take flight.
A realm where silence hums its tune,
Beneath the gaze of a silver moon.

Here blossoms bloom in twilight's glow,
With secrets whispered, soft and low.
The shadows dance on ancient stone,
In this hidden land, we're not alone.

Each petal falls, a promise made,
In twilight's grip, our fears will fade.
The starlit beams, our paths align,
In the realm where shadows intertwine.

With every breath, our spirits rise,
In this enchanted place, no goodbyes.
Where magic stirs with every beat,
And heart and earth so gently meet.

So linger here, where wonders gleam,
In shadows' hush, we find our dream.
Together we'll chase the night's embrace,
In the realm where shadows find their place.

Whispers of Enchanted Marsh

In the misty morn, where shadows play,
Soft whispers linger, guiding the way.
Among the reeds, the secrets unfold,
Of ancient magic, and tales untold.

Frogs croak a symphony, frogs croak a tune,
Beneath the silver light of the moon.
Fireflies dance, like stars in the haze,
Illuminating twilight's gentle phase.

The willows sway with a silky grace,
Embracing the night, a warm embrace.
Each ripple in water tells a tale,
Of forgotten heroes, and their trail.

Secrets of creatures, both small and grand,
Woven together like grains of sand.
A world alive with colors so bright,
In the enchanted marsh, our hearts take flight.

Secrets Beneath the Sorcerer's Shell

In the quiet depths of a shimmering sea,
Lies a magic shell, where none dare to be.
Guarded by whispers of sirens of yore,
Shielding the treasures that lie on the floor.

Beneath the surface, in shadows so deep,
Ancient secrets are wrapped in their sleep.
Silvered currents weave tales of the past,
Of sorcerer's magic, forever to last.

Coral embraces the relics of time,
Each one a memory, a forgotten rhyme.
Legends awaken with each passing tide,
In the heart of the ocean, where dreams can hide.

The bravest of souls may search for the shell,
To uncover the mysteries it holds so well.
Yet, beware the allure that whispers and calls,
For secrets may drown in sorrowful falls.

Shadows on the Verdant Floor

Underneath the canopy, shadows weave,
A tapestry rich, where few dare believe.
Sunlight trickles through leaves overhead,
Painting the ground with colors well-bred.

Among the ferns, where the cool breezes sigh,
Quiet creatures watch as the moments go by.
Moss blankets stones, soft and serene,
Guarding the whispers of what might have been.

Branches embrace in a mystical dance,
While time holds its breath, in a moment's glance.
The whispers of secrets ride on the breeze,
Singing sweet tales that put hearts at ease.

Each step on the earth brings forth a new sound,
Echoing stories held deep in the ground.
In shadows where magic and nature entwine,
Lies a world where the imaginary can shine.

Phantoms of the Glistening Glade

In a glade where moonbeams weave like a thread,
Phantoms of magic dance lightly ahead.
Shimmering figures with laughter so bright,
Filling the night with their enchanting light.

Flowers bloom softly in spectral embrace,
Whispers of dreams linger, leaving a trace.
Glistening dew paints the world with a sigh,
Mirroring stars in the vast velvet sky.

A flicker, a flurry, they scatter and spin,
Eager to share what lies deep within.
Legends and lore of the forest they bring,
Wrapped in the joy that an evening can sing.

In the hush of the night, where shadows may twine,
The glade breathes its secrets, forever divine.
Through whispers and wonders, the phantoms will show,
The heart of the forest, where enchantments grow.

Glimmers of Forgotten Spells

In shadows deep, where whispers dwell,
A flicker sparks, a magic swell.
Forgotten charms within the night,
Awake again, in soft moonlight.

Once woven words in tapestry,
Now dance like leaves, wild and free.
Enchantments drift through secret air,
Calling forth the brave and rare.

A shimmer glows, a memory clear,
Of witches bold who ventured near.
With every step the past unfolds,
In echoes soft, the story holds.

The fireflies weave their slow refrain,
In twilight's grasp, where dreams remain.
The stars above align just right,
To unveil spells lost to the night.

So linger here, let magic soar,
In glimmers bright, forevermore.
For every tale that time forgets,
In heart and mind, the magic sets.

The Hushed Echoes of Ancient Woods

Beneath the boughs where silence creeps,
The ancient woods hold secrets deep.
A rustle there, a whispered sound,
In shadowed glades where dreams abound.

The trees stand tall, their roots entwined,
In stories told, though time confined.
Each leaf a verse, each branch a song,
In tranquil realms where spirits throng.

A gentle breeze lifts memories high,
Of witches' tales beneath the sky.
The mossy stones hold wisdom long,
As echoes rise, both soft and strong.

Amidst the ferns, the spirits play,
In dappled light, where fairies sway.
The forest hums a timeless tune,
As twilight greets the rising moon.

So wander here, let silence guide,
Through ancient woods where secrets hide.
In every breath, the echoes call,
A song of magic, bridging all.

In the Embrace of the Arcane Thicket

In tangled green, where secrets lie,
The thicket whispers, low and shy.
Through twisting vines, the magic flows,
A hidden path where few would go.

With every step, enchantments bloom,
In fragrant air with sweet perfume.
The roots entwined like sorceress' twine,
In this embrace, the worlds align.

A flicker bright, a faerie's glance,
Reveals the dance of night's romance.
With starlit blooms, the shadows sigh,
In harmony, the night draws nigh.

The thicket swells with murmured spells,
In secret glades where wonder dwells.
The mysteries spun in moonlight's thread,
A tapestry of dreams unsaid.

So linger here, where magic spins,
In every breath, the adventure begins.
In the depths of green, hearts entwine,
In the arcane thicket, the stars align.

Twilight's Sorcery in Green Hues

As daylight fades in hues of gold,
The whispers of dusk begin to unfold.
In emerald glades, the shadows creep,
While twilight gathers the earth in sleep.

The trees become a woven cloak,
Where dreams and echoes gently soak.
In silence thick, the magic stirs,
Amidst the leaves, a light that blurs.

Each branch a wand, each star a guide,
In twilight's arms, let wonders bide.
A soft enchantment fills the air,
Like secrets shared, with none to spare.

The fireflies weave their fleeting light,
In the cradle of the enchanting night.
As shadows dance and legends play,
Twilight's sorcery holds sway.

So breathe it in, this twilight's grace,
Let the green hues find their place.
In every dream, let magic run,
In the twilight's glow, we become one.

Tales from the Witches' Vortex

In the heart of the twirling mist,
Whispers of spells in the dusk persist.
Witches gather with bags of lace,
Chanting secrets in a shadowy place.

Stories spun from the threads of night,
Glimmers of magic take their flight.
Potions brewed in cauldrons deep,
Hidden truths that the forest keeps.

Footsteps echo on cobblestones cold,
Tales of the daring and the bold.
An owl's hoot breaks the silence profound,
Mysteries lost and yet to be found.

Around the fire, old ones speak,
Of daring hearts that will not peak.
Curses cast and fortunes told,
Legends alive, forever retold.

The vortex swirls, a dance of fate,
Invite the brave, or seal their state.
For magic thrives where shadows play,
And tales unfold at the break of day.

The Dwelling of Forgotten Charms

In a cottage shrouded by ivy's embrace,
Dusty tomes hold their sacred space.
Whispers of wisdom, a flickering light,
Echoing magic through the lonely night.

Trinkets scattered on shelves piled high,
Each one telling a tale as they sigh.
Cracked mirrors reflect stories untold,
Of brave souls and treasures of old.

A charm that glimmers with stories bright,
Beneath the gaze of the waning twilight.
Time gathered secrets in layers deep,
In the quiet dwelling where shadows creep.

With every breath, an enchantment stirs,
Awakening echoes from long-lost furs.
Memories drift in the candle's glow,
Of lovers and battles from long ago.

Through crumbling halls and winding stairs,
Linger the spirits, the past ensnares.
Here lies the heart of the magical realm,
Where forgotten charms, in silence, overwhelm.

Beneath the Canopy of Enigmas

Beneath the leaves of emerald hue,
Mysteries dance, both old and new.
Threads of fate in the twilight spun,
Secrets whispered when the day is done.

Riddles bloom in the fragrant air,
Each step forward, a daring affair.
Moss carpets hide the lost and found,
Echoes of laughter still abound.

Glimmers of light through branches peak,
The ancients listen, their counsel they seek.
In tangled roots, the answers lie,
Waiting for seekers who dare to try.

With every rustle, a voice awakes,
In the song of the breeze, the heart it takes.
Steps of the brave leave a mark so deep,
In the heart of the forest where secrets sleep.

Enigmas thrive where few would tread,
Among the shadows, where fears are fed.
Yet here is the path for those who dream,
Beneath the canopy, the world may gleam.

A Dance of Luminous Foliage

When autumn flames paint the air bright,
Leaves take flight in a joyous sight.
They swirl like dancers in the breeze,
Whispering stories among the trees.

Golden crowns and scarlet spins,
Nature's ballet where the magic begins.
Each leaf a promise of what has been,
A reflection of wonders, both lost and seen.

The twilight glows with a shimmering sigh,
As the sun dips low in the violet sky.
Footfalls soft on the carpeted ground,
Where echoes of laughter can still be found.

In the moon's embrace, the dance grows bold,
With each twirl, a memory unfolds.
The foliage shimmers with secrets to share,
Of lovers, of friendships, of moments rare.

With every rustle, a heartbeat flows,
In this dance of life, everybody knows.
Luminous foliage, a vibrant trance,
In the heart of the night, we all take a chance.

The Hushed Call of the Faery Pool

In twilight's glow, the waters gleam,
Whispers dance like a fleeting dream.
A fey embrace, so soft and light,
Where shadows play and spirits take flight.

Cascading leaves on the gentle rill,
Echoes of laughter, time stands still.
Moonbeams twine with the cool night air,
As secrets wait with the utmost care.

Around the stones, the nightingale sings,
Of wondrous things and forgotten kings.
Each drop of dew, a tale untold,
In this mystic realm of shimmering gold.

Silken threads weave through nature's lace,
In every whisper, a time-worn trace.
Beneath the stars, hearts intertwine,
In the faery pool, where dreams align.

So linger here, where magic starts,
In hushed murmurs, uncharted arts.
For in this place of eternal grace,
The fae will touch your hidden space.

Echoes of the Spellspring Depths

Where crystal waters weave and swirl,
A world unfolds as secrets twirl.
Beneath the surface, visions bloom,
With every whisper, a hint of doom.

The ancient stones hum a solemn tune,
Carving out paths 'neath the watchful moon.
In tangled roots, the spells are bound,
In every ripple, magic is found.

Elixirs rise from the depths below,
In silvery mists where sparkles flow.
With careful hands, the wise ones glean,
The echoes of what has ever been.

Through wanderlust and daring flight,
The spellspring glimmers, a beacon of light.
Crafted with dreams, so teeny yet grand,
A harmony sung by nature's hand.

Listen close, to the moonlit sound,
Of truths laid bare in the earth's soft ground.
For every stride across this land,
Echoes of magic ever stand.

Dreams Entwined in Verdure

Among the leaves where shadows play,
A tapestry of night meets day.
Roots entwined in a soft embrace,
Bring forth the dreams of a timeless space.

With colors bright, the flowers gleam,
In fragrant whispers, the brave dare dream.
Each petal holds a wish so sweet,
In nature's lap, where hearts can meet.

The gentle sigh of the tender breeze,
Is music sung amongst the trees.
With every rustle, a story flows,
Of hidden lands where wonder grows.

Eyes alight with the morning dew,
As wand'ring souls come into view.
They chase the path where shadows part,
In verdant realms that stir the heart.

So step inside this woven dream,
With laughter bright and starlit beam.
For in this grove, where enchantments twine,
Every moment feels divine.

The Bewitched Soil's Lament

Under the earth, a secret sigh,
Of roots that weave, a whispered cry.
With every grain, a tale unfolds,
In silence deep, the soil beholds.

A dance of words in the fertile clay,
Where echoes linger, fading away.
The shadows deepen, as night descends,
On stories that twist and subtly blend.

In the heart of dusk, a truth thrives,
Each seed, a dream that quietly strives.
Yet burdens weigh on the soil's brow,
As past and present collide somehow.

The tears of rain on the thirsty ground,
Sing softly of lives that swirl around.
In every furrow, a memory's trace,
In the bewitched soil, a lost embrace.

So listen well to the earth's soft plea,
For in its depths, there lies the key.
To stories born from twilight's hands,
In the bewitchment of ancient lands.

The Secret Language of Old Roots

In shadows deep where stories weave,
Old roots converse with whispers low.
Tales of times that few believe,
Secrets shared where soft winds blow.

Beneath the soil, they twist and turn,
Their fibers hold the past's embrace.
In silence, ancient truths still burn,
With every pulse, they trace their grace.

Hushed murmurs heard by listening ears,
Echoes caught in tangled fate.
Through leafy canopies, their fears,
Of time's sharp teeth, they contemplate.

Each gnarled knot a memory kept,
In a dance of life, they intertwine.
Beneath the stars, where shadows leapt,
The roots hold tales of the divine.

So tread with care on this wise ground,
For every step is history's song.
In old roots' rhythm, wisdom found,
A language vast, in silence strong.

Legends Born from Moss and Mire

In the heart of the woods, where the dampness dwells,
Legends arise on the breath of swells.
From soft, emerald moss, and the dark, thick mire,
Whispers of magic, stoked like a fire.

Each droplet caught in the web of light,
Tells tales of the day, soft as the night.
Mysterious creatures, both fierce and shy,
Dance in the shadows, where secrets lie.

Through tangled paths, where few have tread,
Creeping vines cradle what old spirits said.
With every rustle, with each fragile sigh,
New legends are born as the days go by.

Beneath ancient trees, starlight weaves,
A tapestry rich, where the mind believes.
In murky waters, truth lies concealed,
A world unfolded, darkly revealed.

So venture forth, where the wild ones roam,
And find the stories that call you home.
In moss and mire, let your heart align,
With the pulse of the earth, the eternal sign.

Whispers of the Fractal Canopy

In the dance of leaves, where the light breaks free,
Fractals form in harmony.
Whispers weave through branches high,
Nature's voice, a secret sigh.

Through the emerald veil, soft patterns play,
Elders watch from above the fray.
With each rustling leaf, a song is spun,
In the patterns of life, all is one.

The canopy sways in a gentle breeze,
Shadows flicker, and worries ease.
Holding stories from days of old,
In every curve, a dream retold.

Sunlight dapples in gold and green,
A regal dance on the forest's sheen.
Beneath it all, a heartbeat sounds,
The pulse of nature, wherever it bounds.

So listen close to the leaves' soft hum,
In fractal beauty, the answers come.
A world alive in intricate lace,
Whispers of magic in nature's embrace.

The Glistening Veins of Nature's Spell

In hidden groves where the sunlight streams,
Nature weaves her vibrant dreams.
With glistening veins of emerald hue,
A spell of life in every dew.

Each droplet shines like a diamond rare,
Reflecting beauty, beyond compare.
Through winding paths and softest glades,
The treasures of earth, forever cascades.

A symphony played by the rustling brush,
In moments of silence, the world feels hushed.
From roots to skies, all life aligned,
Nature's artwork, both gentle and kind.

Beneath the boughs, a magic flows,
Where every petal and leaf bestows.
In every corner, the wild hearts dwell,
In the glistening veins of nature's spell.

So wander softly with open eyes,
Embrace the wonder that softly lies.
In the threads of life, find joy unmeasured,
In nature's heart, forever treasured.

The Green-Swathed Arcana

In shadows deep, the whispers dwell,
A tapestry of secrets, spun so well.
Leaves that shimmer, pulse with lore,
Beneath the boughs, the spirits soar.

Riddles dance in emerald light,
Mysteries woven, hidden from sight.
Ancient runes on bark engraved,
Guardians watch, the truth enslaved.

Through twilight paths, the wanderers roam,
Finding solace, calling it home.
In every rustle, in every sigh,
The magic lingers, never to die.

With each step, the foliage bends,
As nature's magic never ends.
In the heart of the woods, the arcane waits,
A saga whispered to the fates.

Awake, ye dreamers, seek the soul,
In the green-swathed arcana, feel the whole.
Embrace the secrets the woods impart,
For within their depths lies the heart of art.

Crystals of the Sylvan Abyss

Beneath the mist where shadows creep,
Lie crystals bright, secrets they keep.
Glimmers dance on the water's face,
Echoes whisper in this hidden place.

Branches arch like arms in prayer,
Guarding wonders few would dare.
Each crystal holds a story's spark,
Illuminating the depths of the dark.

The sylvan abyss, a realm of dreams,
Where time flows soft, like silver streams.
Nature's heartbeats, softly entwined,
In the glow of the crystals, magic designed.

Gaze into depths that shimmer and sway,
Where enchantments hide and shadows play.
A treasure trove of the forest's breath,
Revealing beauty, defying death.

So tread with care, and listen close,
For in the silence, the spirits chose.
To share their wisdom, rich and vast,
In the crystals of the sylvan abyss, steadfast.

Unraveled Threads of the Arcane Grove

In a grove where the ancient winds sigh,
Unraveled threads weave tales that fly.
From roots to branches, stories in tow,
Of magic concealed in the twilight glow.

Each thread a whisper, a secret told,
Binding the past in the heart of the old.
Nature's loom spins fabric so fine,
Connecting each soul like ivy entwined.

Glimpse the beauty that time forgot,
In the arcane grove, where dreams are caught.
A patchwork of fables, rich and rare,
A tapestry woven with utmost care.

Dance with the shadows, embrace the night,
Where the stars above ignite the light.
Unraveled threads, a spell they cast,
Uniting the future with echoes past.

Seek the grove, where magic does thrive,
In the delicate web, feel the pulse alive.
In whispers and sighs, the heart will prove,
The depth of the stories in the arcane grove.

Reflections in the Mystic Swamp

In the mystic swamp, where silence reigns,
Reflections shimmer like silver chains.
Moonlight kisses the waters wide,
Revealing worlds that shadows hide.

Amid the reeds, the fireflies twirl,
Painting the night with an endless swirl.
The air is thick with secrets spun,
In the dance of dusk, the magic begun.

Echoes of laughter, long since past,
Whisper through branches, a soft contrast.
Each ripple tells a tale of yore,
Of dreams and wishes forevermore.

With every step, the spirits breathe,
In the mystic swamp, where seekers leave.
A mirror of dreams, or so it seems,
Reflecting the essence of what one dreams.

So linger a while, let go of strife,
In the swamp, embrace the magic of life.
For reflections reveal what the heart can find,
In the serenity of the mystic mind.

The Alchemist's Secret Orchard

In a hidden glade where shadows play,
The fruits of wisdom gleam and sway.
Whispers of magic fill the air,
Each branch a secret waiting there.

Golden apples glisten bright,
Nectar sweet, a wondrous sight.
In this orchard, dreams take flight,
Crafted spells in morning light.

Beneath the boughs, a potion brews,
With every drop, the heart renews.
Here, the brave seek paths anew,
Silent echoes of the true.

An alchemist with hands of flame,
In every pulse, an ancient name.
He guards the key, the mystic lore,
To unlock the heart, forevermore.

But tread with care, for thorns conceal,
A tangled web, the fate we feel.
Through branches thick, the shadows blend,
In this orchard, the journey bends.

Echoing Labyrinths of Thorns

In a maze where shadows twist and weave,
Echoes of sorrow, whispers that cleave.
Thorns entwine in paths so deep,
Secrets buried, memories to keep.

Wanderers lost in despair's embrace,
Searching for light in this darkened place.
Each step taken, a pact with fear,
Every heartbeat invites them near.

Within the thickets, stories reside,
Of hearts once brave that fate defied.
Courage blooms where darkness lies,
In the labyrinth where silence cries.

A flicker glows, a distant spark,
Guiding souls from shadows stark.
With every turn, courage is reborn,
Through echoing paths, the heart is worn.

So tread with caution, but don't lose hope,
For within the thorns lies a way to cope.
The maze may twist, the journey long,
Yet in the struggle, we find our song.

Mysteries Woven in Gossamer Light

In the dawn's embrace, soft and bright,
Whispers of lore dance in the light.
Gossamer threads, so delicate fine,
Weaving their stories in glimmers divine.

Through twilight's veil, the secrets call,
In shimmering threads, we rise or fall.
Each strand a promise, each hue a sigh,
Mysteries held where echoes lie.

A tapestry rich with laughter and tears,
Woven through ages, echoing years.
The fabric of life, both tender and bold,
In gossamer light, our tales unfold.

So gather the threads, let your heart sing,
Embrace the magic that each moment brings.
In the quiet corners where shadows blend,
Mysteries gleam, and dreams ascend.

For in each twinkling, a truth awaits,
To guide the seekers, to open the gates.
In the web of existence, we find our place,
In gossamer light and time's embrace.

Beneath the Canopy of Dreams

Beneath the canopy, stars align,
Whispers of wishes on the vine.
In the stillness, stories take flight,
Bathed in the glow of the moon's soft light.

Dreamers gather, hearts aglow,
In the night air where dreams flow.
Each breath a promise, each glance a thread,
Weaving the visions that dance in our head.

With leaves of silver, the ancient trees,
Hold the secrets of the softest breeze.
Each rustling branch sings a quaint tune,
Inviting the dreams to wander and swoon.

Time stands still in this sacred space,
Where hopes emerge and fears erase.
Beneath the stars, we lay our schemes,
In quiet faith, we dare to dream.

So linger awhile in this enchanted glade,
Where the heart finds rest and time won't fade.
Beneath the canopy, let spirits soar,
In the realm of dreams, forevermore.

Rituals of the Overgrown Crossroads

In shadows deep where whispers creep,
The crossroads halt, where secrets sleep.
With branches twined in gnarled embrace,
The moonlight dances, a spectral grace.

Ancient stones, covered with moss,
Mark the path of the lost, the cross.
Echoes linger, and spirits call,
In dreams persisting, we hear it all.

A flickering flame, an ember's glow,
Illuminates paths where few dare go.
Rituals beckon, with charms unfurled,
A magic hidden, within the world.

Once a year, on the night so still,
The air holds magic, an age-old thrill.
We gather 'round, with hearts ablaze,
A tapestry woven in moonlit haze.

With every chant, the past revives,
In the ancient woods, where mystery thrives.
We dance in circles, the night our guide,
At the overgrown crossroads, where dreams abide.

Secrets Concealed in Foliage

In emerald depths where silence reigns,
Secrets whisper through tangled veins.
Leaves conceal tales of yesteryear,
In every rustle, a truth draws near.

Hidden paths in a sun-dappled glade,
Where shadows play and memories fade.
The air is thick with enchantment's breath,
Life abounds, and so does death.

The roots entwine like lovers lost,
In the heart of the wood, we pay the cost.
For every secret, a price must be,
In the foliage cloak, what will we see?

A glimmer of gold, a fleeting glance,
In the underbrush, we take our chance.
With every step, the forest sighs,
Unveiling wonders before our eyes.

In silence we ponder, in wonder we tread,
In nature's embrace, by secrets led.
Concealed in the leaves, life's dance unfolds,
A timeless tale, in whispers told.

When the Wildflowers Speak

When wildflowers bloom in riotous hue,
They tell of the skies, the sun, the dew.
Petals open like mouths in cheer,
Their voices rise, for all to hear.

In fields of gold and waves of blue,
They beckon hearts, both old and new.
With fragrance sweet, they weave a song,
A melody bright, inviting us along.

Every blossom bears a tale to share,
Of summer's warmth and whispered air.
Beneath their grace, the world awakes,
In each soft flutter, a promise breaks.

They beckon children to dance and play,
In harmony with the close of day.
And when they sway in gentle breeze,
A symphony dwells among the trees.

So heed their call when the sunlight streams,
In the language of blooms, we find our dreams.
When wildflowers speak, let your spirit roam,
In the petals' song, you'll find your home.

Tales from the Verdant Abyss

In the verdant abyss where shadows blend,
Tales of old and new transcend.
Beneath the canopy, secrets thrive,
A hidden world where magic's alive.

The brook's soft murmur, a timeless verse,
Carries stories from the universe.
Among the ferns and moss-kissed stones,
History breathes in chill and tones.

Whispers float on the cool night air,
As creatures gather without a care.
Each heartbeat of nature resonates,
In the stillness, destiny waits.

The brambles hide a treasure chest,
Of memories woven, life's great quest.
In twilight's glow, we seek to find,
The stories etched in the leaves entwined.

So let us wander, with hearts set free,
In the abyss, where we long to be.
For in shadows deep, we find our part,
Tales of the wild, spoken from the heart.

The Chalice of Verdant Illusion

In twilight's shade, where whispers bloom,
A chalice waits, in nature's room.
With emerald glints and secrets deep,
It holds the dreams that ancient keep.

Underneath the canopy's embrace,
Mystic visions dance with grace.
Each drop a tale, of love and lore,
Inviting hearts to seek for more.

From roots entwined in stories told,
To silver ferns, both brave and bold.
The winds would weave their softest song,
In this green realm where dreams belong.

Yet shadows lurk where light may wane,
A choice to bear, a hint of pain.
To sip or not, to take the leap,
Into the depths where wonders sleep.

So gather close, in circles tight,
And let the chalice spark your flight.
For in the heart of nature's guise,
Lies the magic that never dies.

Resonance of the Hidden Boughs

Beneath the trees, where echoes dwell,
A symphony of secrets swell.
The boughs above in whispers twine,
A dance of shadows, soft, divine.

In every flicker, sight concealed,\nResonance of the forest
revealed.
A rhythm pulses, vibrant, pure,
The ancient woods continue to lure.

With every rustle and gentle sway,
The hidden paths invite to stray.
In emerald hues the spirits play,
Guiding wanderers who find their way.

Yet heed the call, both fierce and sweet,
For magic stirs at nature's feet.
In thickets lush and wild embrace,
The heart can find its rightful place.

So linger long in twilight's hold,
And listen to the tales of old.
For in the rustling leaves of night,
Lies harmony, both bright and slight.

Among the Sylvan Shimmers

Among the shimmers, soft and clear,
Where sunlight kisses green and dear.
The forest gleams with jeweled beams,
And every glance ignites our dreams.

In dappled light, the fairies play,
Their laughter like the break of day.
With petals pink and sapphire skies,
They weave the worlds beyond our eyes.

Through ferny paths, the wild things roam,
In nature's clasp, they find their home.
Each rustling leaf, a gentle sound,
In this embrace, true peace is found.

The brooklet hums a silvery tune,
Reflecting whispers of the moon.
Yet silence calls, a voice so deep,
In sylvan hues, enchantments sleep.

So wander close with heart attuned,\nAmong the
shimmers, be marooned.
For in this realm, where magic swells,
The forest holds its myriad spells.

Beneath Twilight's Green Veil

Beneath the veil of twilight's hue,
The earth awaits, both fresh and new.
With sighs of night, the shadows creep,
While secrets in the silence sleep.

The stars emerge, a tender grace,
Illuminating nature's face.
In whispered tones, the crickets sing,
Their chorus heralding the spring.

With every breeze, a tale unfurls,
Of hidden realms, and ancient pearls.
The twilight wrapped in emerald lace,
Invites the wanderers to embrace.

In hush of dusk, the world feels right,
As magic blooms in soft twilight.
A gentle touch, a fleeting glance,
To seek the heart, to find the dance.

So linger long, where dreams delight,
In twilight's charm, both pure and bright.
For beneath the green, the heart can dwell,
In whispered tales, where magic swells.

The Enigmatic Pulse of the Glade

In the heart of the glade, whispers twine,
Secrets hold sway where the shadows align.
Dappled light dances on leaves green and gold,
Mysteries thrive in the silence untold.

Creatures of magic flit soft through the air,
Their laughter like chimes, both joyful and rare.
Beneath ancient oaks, time seems to bend,
Threads of enchantment that never shall end.

With each gentle breeze, the trees seem to sigh,
Guardians of wonders and wishes gone by.
Echoes of dreams in a world so alive,
Here in this haven, the heart learns to thrive.

Moonlit reflections on waters that gleam,
Crickets compose a harmonious dream.
The pulse of the glade weaves stories anew,
Of magic and nature, forever in view.

In twilight's embrace, the night softly calls,
The glade holds its secrets within ancient walls.
Alluring, enchanting, a place to behold,
The Enigmatic Pulse, where legends unfold.

Fragments of a Forgotten Spellbook

Tattered pages wait in a dusty old nook,
Whispers of magic within the spellbook.
Flickering candles cast shadows that sway,
Guiding the seeker lost in dismay.

Words like a lilt drift through the cool air,
Carrying wisdom and wonder to share.
Each line a portal to realms far away,
A glimpse of the magic that once held its sway.

Curled leaves of parchment, ink fading with time,
Echo a language both ancient and sublime.
Mysteries bloom from each carefully penned,
A tapestry woven where past meets the end.

An artist once crafted with elegant grace,
The symbols of power etched in their place.
Fingers trace passages written in ink,
Unlocking the secrets that cause hearts to think.

As shadows all deepen, enchantments are spun,
Fragments of lore dance as darkness is done.
In a world still alive where dreams twirl and gleam,
The forgotten spellbook ignites every dream.

The Sorcerer's Verdant Lair

Nestled in thickets where secrets entwine,
A sorcerer's home, where shadows recline.
Vines curl around each well-worn stone wall,
Guarding the wonders that beckon to all.

Potions a-glimmer in glass jars align,
Herbs fragrant and rich in the cool, ancient shrine.
Whispers of magic thread softly through air,
Promising visions and promises rare.

Under the boughs of a towering tree,
Incantations linger, both wild and free.
Moonlight spills down like a silken embrace,
Shrouding the lair with serenades' grace.

Stars twinkle brightly, a celestial chart,
Guiding the wise with the magic of heart.
In solitude's shelter, the dreams intertwine,
Spinning adventures in the depths of the pine.

With every soft rustle, each creature, each leaf,
Speaks tales of journeys beyond ev'ry grief.
The Sorcerer's Lair, lush, vibrant, and bold,
A refuge for magics and wonders untold.

Beneath Shadowed Ferns

Under the ferns where the wild whispers rise,
A realm filled with lore beneath twilight skies.
Soft petals dance in the hush of the night,
Veiling the glimmers of soft, silver light.

Crickets compose a chorus so sweet,
Singing of journeys where earth and dreams meet.
Each leaf a canvas for stories unfurled,
In the tapestry woven of magic and world.

With shadows that cradle the secrets they keep,
Every heartbeat echoes in rhythms so deep.
Beneath shadowed fronds, the heart finds its tune,
A soft serenade 'neath the watchful moon.

Mystical fungi, like stars that have fallen,
Glow softly in darkness, like night's gentle callin'.
Nature whispers wisdom to those who will pause,
Inviting the curious to ponder its laws.

In quiet repose, the world holds its breath,
Beneath shadowed ferns, the dance of enchantments.
Where magic awaits in each graceful embrace,
A sanctuary found, a nurturing space.

www.ingramcontent.com/pod-product-compliance
Ingram Content Group UK Ltd.
Pitfield, Milton Keynes, MK11 3LW, UK
UKHW022005200125
4187UKWH00037B/895